STEP-UP
RELIGION

How do the beliefs of Christians influence their actions?

Jean Mead and Ruth Nason

Evans

Published by Evans Brothers Limited
2A Portman Mansions
Chiltern Street
London W1U 6NR

© Evans Brothers Limited 2008

Produced for Evans Brothers Limited by
White-Thomson Publishing Ltd,
Bridgewater Business Centre,
210 High Street,
Lewes, East Sussex BN7 2NH

Printed in China by New Era Printing Co. Ltd.

Project manager: Ruth Nason

Designer: Helen Nelson at Jet the Dog

British Library Cataloguing in Publication Data

Mead, Jean

How do the beliefs of Christians influence their
actions? - (Step-up religion)

1. Christian life - Juvenile literature

I. Title II. Nason, Ruth

248.4

ISBN-13: 9780237534103

Acknowledgements

The Author and Publishers are grateful to Sue
Ridge of Little Heath Primary School, Potters Bar,
for her advice on the teachers' page; Class 5 of
Immanuel and St Andrew Primary School, Lambeth,
for their class rules; Jen Lynch; and members and
children from Blackhorse Road Baptist Church,
Walthamstow, for their help and willingness to be
photographed, especially Gillian Moyles and
Norman Coe.

Photographs are from: Alamy: pages 6 (Janine
Wiedel Photolibrary), 19 (Aliki Sapountzi/aliki
image library), 21 (Bubbles Photolibrary); City of
Westminster Archives Centre: page 18b; Corbis:
cover (main) (Sucheta Das/Reuters), pages 1/8
(Reuters), 7 (Bettmann), 9b (Archivo Iconografico,
S.A.), 17 (Kapoor Baldev), 18t (Bill Tarrant/Reuters),
20 (Tim Pannell), 24 (P. Deliss/Godong); Getty
Images: pages 13, 15 (AFP); iStockphoto.com:
pages 4tl (Valerie Loiseleux), 9t (Joseph C.
Justice Jr); Jean Mead: cover tr, pages 4tr, 4br,
5, 11l, 12, 16, 22, 26, 27t, 27b; Michael Nason:
page 10; Tearfund/David Bainbridge: page 27c;
Topfoto.co.uk: cover tl, pages 4t (EMPICS), 4bl (The
Image Works), 11r, (Topham/Woodmansterne), 23
(EE Images/HIP), 25 (UPP).

Contents

Difficult decisions

We all have difficult decisions to make sometimes. What do you think the people here should do? What difficult decisions or choices have you made?

It can be hard, deciding things in parliament. For example, should we say yes to building nuclear power stations, to provide the electricity our country needs?

I promised my brother not to tell of him stealing, but I'm worried. What should I do?

My gran gave me a present that's babyish. Should I tell her the truth or pretend that I love the present?

Should I give my daughter what she likes best, even though I know it's not very good for her?

I'd like some trainers like my friend's, but I've heard that they're made in factories where people are paid unfair wages. Should I buy the trainers anyway?

Why is it difficult to decide?

It can be difficult to decide what to do when:

- There are many things to choose from.

- There is something that you want to do, but you know it will have some bad effects.

- You don't have enough information about all sides of a question or situation.

- Other people are trying to persuade you to do something.

- Ideas about right and wrong could lead you to do two different things. For example, you believe that you should be kind and also truthful, but sometimes telling the truth would hurt someone.

What influences you?

Think of a choice or decision that you have made. Which of the following influenced you?

- I knew I could be punished if I did the wrong thing.

- The rules I have learnt at home and at school.

- The people around me and what they do.

- My feelings (for example, anger, love, fear, excitement).

- I believe that people should be kind to each other.

- My conscience. I knew I would feel guilty if I did the wrong thing.

- The beliefs and teachings of my religion.

The golden rule

Many religions teach the idea: Treat others as you would like to be treated. This is called the golden rule. How would this rule help the people on page 4 to decide what to do?

◀ *What do you think makes someone behave kindly? Christians may be influenced by Jesus's saying: 'Do to others as you would have them do to you.' Many other people also use this saying as a motto to guide their behaviour.*

Rules and values

At school, have you agreed some rules, like the 'Golden Behaviours' (right) written by one Year Five class? What effect do the rules have on how it feels in the classroom?

A law is a rule that the government has agreed for the whole country. If someone is accused of breaking a law, there may be a court case to decide if they are guilty. If the person is found guilty, a judge or a magistrate decides the punishment.

▼ *There are rules for everyone who uses the roads and pavements, in the Highway Code. Which of these rules do you know? Would it work to replace the Highway Code with one general rule, such as: Be polite and don't do anything dangerous?*

😊 Our Class Golden Behaviours

1. Listen to people when they are talking.
2. Keep your hands under control.
3. Respect people and their property.
4. Keep your language and actions polite and kind.
5. Sharing is important.
6. Do put up your hand if you have a request or question.
7. Use your opportunities well.
8. Do concentrate on your work.
9. Keep the learning environment tidy.
10. Walk around the school sensibly.

If you follow instructions and keep these Golden Behaviours, you're on the right track!

Sometimes people talk about an 'unwritten rule' or 'the done thing'. This means a custom that people follow because they seem to agree that it is right. It's an unwritten rule that people give each other presents on special occasions, or that people queue to wait for something. Can you think of other examples?

Laws, rules and customs help us to decide what to do.

Basic beliefs or values

Laws and rules are often based on general beliefs about what is important, such as:

- All people are equally important.

- People should be free to believe what they want.

- We should try to live peacefully.

- We should look after the world so that other people can enjoy it.

Which of these general beliefs or values are behind your classroom rules? Which basic beliefs influence you in what you do?

Is it always right to follow rules?

It is usually right to obey rules and laws, but not always. A rule may be wrong and unfair. Some states of the USA used to have laws that kept black people apart from white people. For example, black people were only allowed to sit at the back of buses. People began to break these laws, in protest against their unfairness. Eventually the government changed the laws.

It takes courage to challenge a law, knowing that you could be punished for breaking it. But sometimes this may be the only way to get bad laws changed.

The 'why?' game

Ask someone to say what they are doing, and why. Then, in response to their answer, ask them why again. How many 'why?'s do you need to ask before you discover one of the person's deep general beliefs or values? Try this with several people and make a list of the basic values you discover.

▲ In the 1960s, these Americans deliberately broke the law by sitting together in a bus station waiting room that was for white people only. In this way, they showed their belief that such rules were wrong and should be changed.

Christian beliefs and values

This book is going to look at what Christians believe, and how this influences the way they live and what they do. Christian beliefs and values come from the life and teaching of Jesus.

Who is Jesus, for Christians?

Jesus lived about 2,000 years ago, in the land that is now Israel. He and the people among whom he lived were Jewish. Jesus taught people about God, and how God wants people to behave, based on ideas in the Jewish Bible.

▼ *Jesus told his followers to spread his teachings, and many Christians think this is an important thing to do. Following Jesus and his teaching about God's love makes them feel happy, and so they want to pass this on.*

The Jewish Bible tells how the Jewish people became 'God's people'. God promised to care for them, and they promised to obey God. But Christians believe that, eventually, God sent Jesus to the world, to show that God is ready to love and care for any person at all who loves God and turns to God for help.

Christians believe that Jesus was God's son, born as a human on Earth. Jesus showed what human beings can be like if they trust God and live as God wishes. Christians therefore try to follow the example of Jesus.

Jesus died on a cross, but Christians believe that he came alive again and returned to live with God for ever. This leads Christians to feel that Jesus is alive now, loving and helping them in their lives. They also believe that, by his death, Jesus made it possible for anyone to have life after death with God.

The Bible

Christians read about Jesus and his teachings in the Bible, which is divided into the Old Testament and the New Testament. The Old Testament was written before Jesus was born. It is almost the same as the Jewish Bible that Jesus knew. It contains the commandments that God gave to the Jewish leader Moses, to show how God's people should live. These include the Ten Commandments, such as: 'You shall not steal' and 'Honour your father and mother.'

The Old Testament traces the history of God's people, including many events in which it was difficult to stay obedient to God. Stories show how some people found the strength to do what God asked them to do.

Christians read all parts of the Bible to help them to think how to obey God in their lives. Some try to follow exactly what the Bible says. Others interpret it more for modern times.

The New Testament begins with four books called gospels, about the life and teaching of Jesus. Other books in the New Testament show how Jesus's first followers spread his teachings. They include letters from a Christian called Paul, helping groups of new Christians to follow the religion.

Why do people disobey?

Read the story of Adam and Eve, in a children's Bible (Genesis 2 and 3). Talk with a friend about why you think Adam and Eve disobeyed God's rule. What makes you disobey rules or instructions sometimes?

The Old Testament tells how God created Adam and Eve, the first humans, who lived with God in a beautiful garden. God told them not to eat fruit from the tree of knowledge of good and evil, but they disobeyed. God therefore sent them away from the garden.

What did Jesus say about rules?

Like other Jewish people, Jesus learned about God's laws and commandments in the Jewish Bible. There were hundreds of laws about many aspects of daily life, but the two basic ones were:

▶ *This stained glass picture in a church shows Jesus as a young boy in the temple, talking with religious leaders about the Jewish law.*

- 'Love the Lord your God with all your heart and with all your soul and with all your strength and with all your mind.'

- 'Love your neighbour as yourself.'

Like the Jewish religious leaders and experts, Jesus said that keeping these two laws is the way to please God. The two laws sum up the values by which Christians live.

Does keeping laws make a person good?

Jesus and the Jewish religious leaders agreed about the two basic laws, but there was a big debate about how to put them into practice. Some religious leaders criticised Jesus for breaking Jewish laws and traditions. Jesus said that simply keeping all the rules does not make a person good. He pointed out that a person may act correctly and appear good, but their thoughts and motives may not be good. Can you think of a modern example of that? It is sometimes called hypocrisy.

◀ *Does it matter if you talk unkindly about a person, as long as you are not actually unkind? Jesus said that unkind talk comes from evil thoughts, and that God cares most about a person's thoughts.*

Making some rules harder

Jesus gave people new ideas about God's laws, which made some of them harder to follow. For example, Jesus said that it was not enough just to keep the commandment, 'Do not murder.' To please God, people must not even have hateful thoughts about someone. Similarly, Jesus said that it was not enough just to 'love your neighbour'. God wanted people to love their enemies as well.

Jesus and Zaccheus

Some Jewish people looked down on and avoided people who did not follow God's laws. Therefore they were shocked when Jesus made friends with such people – for example, the tax collector Zaccheus, who made himself rich by cheating people. But when Jesus was friendly to Zaccheus, Zaccheus changed. He gave all the money he had kept for himself to help the poor.

▲ *Jesus showed the idea of 'loving your enemies' when he met Zaccheus. Which parts of the story from Luke 19: 1-10 are shown in this medieval Bible illustration? How do you think the story might influence what Christians do today?*

Jesus and Zaccheus

Draw and write the story of Zaccheus as a comic strip, with some thought bubbles as well as speech bubbles. Decide on a good title.

Putting beliefs into practice

Jesus said that everyone who lives as God wants will be part of the Kingdom of God. He told people to make themselves ready for the beginning of this Kingdom, and he said that the way to be ready is to act on his teachings.

Jesus often used stories called parables to tell people about his ideas. The parable of the wise and foolish builders (right) is about putting Jesus's teachings into practice.

The wise and foolish builders

Everyone who hears my teachings and puts them into practice is like a wise man who built his house on rock. A storm came but the house stood firm.

Everyone who hears my teachings and does not put them into practice is like a foolish man who built his house on sand. In the storm, the house crashed down. (Luke 6: 46-49)

Jesus told his followers that their actions should show what type of people they are, just as the fruit that grows on a tree shows what type of tree it is. Christians therefore believe that it is very important for their beliefs to influence what they do, and for their lives to show something about what they believe.

▲ Christians get together in groups and in churches, to read the Bible and help each other to learn about and follow Jesus's teachings.

A tree of actions

Draw a large picture of a tree. Among the roots, write one of your basic beliefs. In the branches, display pictures that show how you and other people put that belief into practice.

Teachings to follow

So far we have seen these teachings of Jesus, which Christians try to put into practice:

- Trust God and live as God wishes.

- Love God, and love your neighbour as yourself.

- Do not have hateful thoughts about anyone.

- Love your enemies.

- Show these basic values in the way you live.

What does it mean to trust God?

To explain how people should trust God to care for them, Jesus said:

> Why do you worry about clothes? See how lilies grow in the field. If that is how God clothes the grass of the field, will he not much more clothe you?
> (Matthew 6: 28-30)

Jesus said that it is very difficult for people to trust God in this way. He told the parable of the rich fool (right) to show that it doesn't work to trust your own efforts and possessions to make you happy.

▲ How might Christians put Jesus's teachings into practice when the shops are full of things to buy at Christmas?

The parable of the rich fool

A rich man owned fields that produced wonderful crops. He decided to build a huge barn to store all his grain and belongings. Then he could take life easy, with no worries, and eat, drink and be merry.

But God said, 'You foolish man! This night you will die, and then who will get all the things you have stored for yourself?'
(Luke 12: 16-21)

To update the parable for today, what type of rich person and belongings would you describe?

The parable of the good Samaritan

In the gospel of Luke, Christians read that an expert in Jewish law questioned Jesus about the law to 'Love your neighbour as yourself' (see page 10). The man asked Jesus, 'Who is my neighbour?' To answer him, Jesus told the parable of the good Samaritan. A Samaritan was a person from the country of Samaria.

This parable was shocking to Jesus's Jewish listeners, because it showed a Samaritan to be kinder than a Jewish priest and a Jewish temple official, called a Levite. At the time of Jesus, Jewish people despised Samaritans, because they were from a different race and religion, and Samaritans hated Jews.

The good Samaritan

A Jewish man was making his way along the dangerous road from Jerusalem to Jericho, when he was attacked and robbed. The robbers left him at the roadside, half-dead.

First a priest and then a Levite from the Jewish temple walked past. They did not stop to help the man.

But a Samaritan man did stop to look after him. He bandaged the man's wounds and took him on his donkey to an inn, where he cared for the man overnight.

In the morning, the Samaritan asked the innkeeper to look after the injured man while he was away. He gave the innkeeper some money and said he would pay him more if necessary when he returned.
(Luke 10: 25-37)

▲ *This carving of the good Samaritan is in Rochester Cathedral. The Latin words mean 'Go and do likewise.'*

After telling the story, Jesus asked, 'Which of the three passers-by was a neighbour to the man who was attacked?' The expert in Jewish law answered, 'The one who helped him.'

Jesus said, 'Go and do likewise.' In other words, be kind and help all people in need, no matter who they are. See them and treat them as human beings, the same as yourself. This teaching of Jesus leads many Christians to make helping the needy an important part of their lives.

▶ *In 2007, some holiday-makers on the island of Tenerife helped to care for some migrants who landed on the beach, exhausted and unwell, after a dangerous sea journey from Africa. Could you base a modern version of the good Samaritan story on this?*

Helping people in need

What thoughts do you think were in the minds of the people in the parable of the good Samaritan? Try to make a list of thoughts that would lead a person to walk by without helping, and another list of thoughts that would make a person decide to help. What makes it difficult to help? What is the strongest reason for helping?

Why do Christians help the needy?

Jesus taught, 'Love your neighbour as yourself' and 'Love your enemies' too. In his actions and in his teachings, he showed that it is right to treat all people with kindness and care. But the answer to 'Why do Christians help the needy?' is not simply 'because Jesus taught that God wants people to be kind and loving'.

Love comes from God

Christians believe that all love comes from God. God created people to be able to love, like God. In one of the letters in the New Testament, a Christian called John explains this idea: 'We [humans] love because God first loved us.'

Christians also believe that God sent his son Jesus to the world, so that people would understand how much God loves them.

These beliefs mean that Christians love others because they feel so loved by God. They believe that it is God's love in them that causes them to help people in need.

Homeless teenagers need a safe place to live. I believe I should share what I have.

▲ *Jen enjoys helping a scheme called 'Crash pad' for 16-17 year olds who are homeless. She welcomes the young people into her home, providing a bedroom and meals. Jen is 80, but still works as a music teacher. Do you think her belief about sharing influences her work too?*

The Salvation Army

Find out about the beliefs and actions of the Salvation Army. Go to www.salvationarmy.org.uk/schools, click on 'kids' and download the pack on 'Faith in action'.

Mother Teresa

A Roman Catholic nun called Mother Teresa (1910-97) was a Christian who devoted her life to caring for the poor. First she started an open-air school for slum children in Calcutta, India. This led to her founding an order of nuns called the Missionaries of Charity. They now provide practical care to the poorest people in many countries.

Mother Teresa said that she was influenced by the words of Jesus in a Bible passage (right) from Matthew 25: 31-46. From this passage Christians understand that Jesus thought of all people as his 'brothers' and that, in some way, Jesus shares people's suffering. He wants his followers to show their love for him by treating other people as if they were Jesus.

What examples can you think of today of people who are hungry, thirsty, strangers, in need of clothes, sick and in prison? What could you do to help?

◀ Mother Teresa said: 'Suffering today is because people are hoarding, not giving, not sharing.' What do you think?

The sheep and the goats

Jesus said that, at the end of time, the Son of Man (a name for Jesus) will sit on his throne and separate all the people into two groups, as a shepherd separates sheep from goats.

As King, he will say to one group: 'Come, take the kingdom prepared for you since the creation of the world. For I was hungry and you gave me something to eat, I was thirsty and you gave me something to drink, I was a stranger and you invited me in, I needed clothes and you clothed me, I was sick and you looked after me, I was in prison and you came to visit me.'

These people will ask when they did all these things for him, and he will say: 'Whatever you did for one of the least of these brothers of mine, you did for me.'

The other group gave no help to people in need. They will go away to eternal punishment.

How do Christians help the needy?

Christians believe that helping others is one of the most important things that God wants them to do. This belief may inspire a Christian to give money to a charity, or to give time and skills to do charity work.

Examples from history

In history lessons, you may have learnt about some Christians who helped the needy. In medieval times, monasteries cared for the sick. The first hospitals developed from this.

In Victorian times, the industrial revolution led to poverty and hardship for many working people. Lord Shaftesbury (1801-85) was an MP who campaigned for new laws to protect children working in factories and mines. Thomas Barnardo (1845-1905) set up homes for street children. Like many Victorian reformers, Shaftesbury and Barnardo were Christians who believed that they should help the needy and lead more people to become Christian. What can you find out about the modern charities named after these men?

▲ These volunteers for a Christian organisation called Service International went to Sri Lanka to help build houses for people whose homes were destroyed by the tsunami in 2005.

▶ The Victorian reformer Lord Shaftesbury (in the background, left) helped to set up many 'ragged schools', making it possible for the first time for the poorest children to go to school. He was inspired by his Christian beliefs.

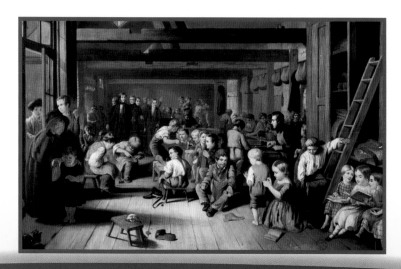

Examples in churches

If you visit an old church, look for a plaque or board about a local person who gave money to help the poor and needy.

The people at many churches today organise help for the needy in the neighbourhood, such as providing meals for the homeless, driving elderly people to hospital appointments and listening to people who want to talk about their problems. Churches also make links with people in need in other places, including other countries. At a local church, look for posters and notices about the charity work that the church members do and support.

Christian charities

There are many charities run by Christians. Some are connected with particular denominations of Christianity. Charities provide help when there is a natural disaster, or other emergency, and where there is continuing need. Many charities aim to enable people to help themselves, for example by giving them useful equipment. They may teach practical skills and send volunteers to help with the labour.

Charity logos

Find out what logos are used by Christian charities such as Christian Aid, CAFOD, Tearfund and World Vision. What symbols are used in the logos? Make up a logo for a charity that you would like to set up.

Some charities work to persuade governments to change laws that make it difficult for poverty to be ended. The charity Christian Aid says:

'We strive for a new world transformed by an end to poverty and we campaign to change the rules that keep people poor.'

Christians support Christian charities by giving money, doing voluntary work, and joining in campaigns. They also pray for God's help for the charity and its workers.

◀ *Many Christian charities are part of the 'Make Poverty History' campaign, which began in 2005.*

Do to others as you would have them do to you

How do you like people to treat you? Do you agree with this list and what would you add?

I like it when someone:

- remembers what I like
- shares something with me
- helps me to do something difficult
- trusts me to do something on my own
- respects my point of view
- tells me the truth
- laughs at my jokes
- says 'well done!'

Choose three of the ways that you like to be treated and think of examples of when you have treated other people in those ways. Is it difficult sometimes, and if so, why?

A basic rule for everyone

Christians think of Jesus's words, 'Love your neighbour as yourself' and 'Do to others as you would have them do to you.' But other religions have similar teachings. For example, the Jewish Bible contains a verse, 'What you hate, do not do to anyone.' The Hindu scriptures say, 'Don't do to others that which,

◀ *How do you think this boy feels with everyone saying 'well done'? How can you make someone feel special?*

if done to you, would cause you pain.' Part of the Sikh holy book says, 'As you regard yourself, so regard others.' Probably most people, whether they follow a religion or not, have a basic belief that it is right to treat other people as you would like them to treat you.

What to do or what not to do?

'Don't treat others in ways that you wouldn't like.' Does that mean the same as 'Treat others as you would like to be treated'? Think of examples to help you to decide.

How love influences actions

Do you remember, from page 16, that Christians believe that love comes from God? A Bible passage about love is from one of Paul's letters. Paul says that having love for others leads people to treat others in certain ways:

> Love is patient and kind. It does not envy, it does not boast, it is not proud. It is not rude, it is not self-seeking, it is not easily angered, it keeps no record of wrongs. Love does not delight in evil but rejoices with the truth. It always protects, always trusts, always hopes, always perseveres.
> (1 Corinthians 13: 4-7)

What if you are treated wrongly?

Jesus said these surprising things about what to do if someone treats you wrongly:

> If someone strikes you on one cheek, let them strike the other cheek too.
>
> If someone takes your coat, don't stop them from taking your tunic too.
>
> If someone takes what belongs to you, do not ask for it back. (Luke 6: 29-30)

What different things might people choose to do in the situations above? How would doing what Jesus said affect what happened next? Do you think that perhaps Jesus was saying, 'Don't try to get your own back'?

▼ *What do you think it's best to do when someone hurts you or makes you angry?*

Forgiveness

Can you think of an example of when you felt angry with someone for something they did? The example below is from one of the authors of this book.

Have I forgiven him?

I came home to find my husband working in the garden. To make more space, he had cut off all the bottom branches of a large bush. I was horrified. It was my favourite bush. It stayed green and had flowers on all through winter. Now it looked silly, with a long bare trunk and a few branches at the top. I cried and became angry with my husband. He said he had only been trying to help and that he thought the garden looked better now.

I didn't stay cross for very long. We 'made up' and laughed about it. And yet every now and then, when I see the bush, I feel upset again and say how horrid I think it looks.

When I said I was writing about forgiveness, my husband suggested that I put in this story.

You could try writing the story from the point of view of the author's husband. Or describe your own example from the point of view of the person you were angry with.

Forgiving someone for something means saying, 'It's fine. Don't let's think about it any more,' and behaving as though it had never happened. What would you say 'being forgiven' means?

What do you think it feels like to be forgiven? What do you think a person feels like if they are not forgiven?

▼ Shaking hands is a gesture that can mean 'All is forgiven.' Forgiveness brings people together again.

God's forgiveness

Jesus taught that God always forgives anyone who asks to be forgiven. To show what it is like when someone turns back to God and is forgiven, Jesus told the parable of the lost son.

In the parable, in Luke 15: 11-32, a father has two sons. One of them leaves home with his share of his father's money, spends it all on himself, and ends up in a job feeding pigs, so poor and hungry that he longs to eat the pigs' food. At last, he decides to go home, say sorry, and ask his father to employ him as a servant.

The father sees his son coming home and runs out joyfully to meet him. He gives his son fine clothes and arranges a feast to celebrate because, he says, 'My son was dead and is alive again. He was lost and is found!'

What words do you think the son would use to describe how it felt to be received like that?

▲ *This picture of Jesus's death on the cross, called the Crucifixion, is in a church in India. Around the picture are words that Jesus spoke before he died (Luke 23: 34). Christians believe that, through his death, Jesus took the punishment for the wrongdoing of everyone in the world, so that it became possible for God to forgive everyone who asks. They believe that all people can be forgiven and, by following Jesus, live forever with God.*

An acrostic poem

Remember a time when you were forgiven and write an acrostic poem about it, starting each line with the next letter of the word 'FORGIVEN'.

Being forgiving

Peter, one of Jesus's followers, asked Jesus how many times he should forgive someone. Jesus said 'seventy times seven' (Matthew 18: 21-22). He meant an endless number of times.

Jesus also told his followers that they should be forgiving, as God is forgiving. To show this idea, he told the parable of the unforgiving servant (right). In the parable, the king is like God.

▲ In the Lord's Prayer, Christians pray to God: 'Forgive us our sins, as we forgive those who sin against us.' Christians also ask God to help them when they find it difficult to forgive.

The unforgiving servant

A king wanted his servants to pay back the money they owed him. One servant owed £10,000 and could not repay it. The king ordered that his family should be sold as slaves, to raise the money.

But the servant pleaded with the king, his master, to give him more time to repay the debt. The king took pity on him and cancelled the debt completely.

Then the servant grabbed a fellow-servant and demanded back £10 that he owed him. He ignored the fellow-servant's plea for time and had him thrown into prison.

The king heard about this and said, 'I cancelled that enormous debt of yours. Shouldn't you have forgiven your fellow-servant, as I forgave you?' The king was angry and had the first servant imprisoned until he could pay back all of his debt. (Matthew 18: 23-34)

Like the parable of the lost son (page 23), the parable of the unforgiving servant shows that God's forgiveness is limitless. The servant owed his master the largest amount of money that could be imagined in Jesus's time. The parable also shows that God expects people to echo his forgiveness.

Some Christians understand that the end of the parable means that God will not forgive them if they are unforgiving towards anyone. Matthew's gospel says that, after telling the parable, Jesus warned: 'This is how God will treat you unless you forgive your fellows from your heart.' What do you think Christians understand by 'from the heart'?

Putting the teaching into practice

Forgiveness is a very important subject in Christian belief. Christians try to be forgiving in their treatment of people, and in their thoughts about people.

Sometimes you hear about forgiveness on the television news. For example, when people have been killed, the news reporters may interview relatives, who say that they

Stories of forgiveness

Read some real-life examples of forgiveness at www.theforgivenessproject. com. Think if there is something you could forgive, and what to do about it.

Why do you look at the speck of sawdust in your brother's eye and pay no attention to the plank in your own eye?
(Luke 6: 41)

▲ What do these words of Jesus tell Christians about criticising other people?

forgive, or that they cannot forgive, the killers. Some of the people interviewed are Christians.

Truly forgiving someone is not easy, and Christians discuss whether some things are so bad that Jesus would not tell them to forgive the people who are responsible. Julie Nicholson, a vicar whose daughter was killed by a terrorist's bomb, felt unable to feel forgiveness. She felt that she could only leave that to God.

◄ Former South African archbishop Desmond Tutu is well-known for his ideas about forgiveness. He has said: 'When I talk of forgiveness I mean the belief that you can come out the other side a better person. A better person than the one being consumed by anger and hatred.'

DESMOND TUTU
NO FUTURE WITHOUT FORGIVENESS

What difference does it make?

This book has shown some of the beliefs that influence Christians. Christians believe that God loves them and knows all about them. They trust God always to care for them, and to forgive them.

Christians believe that God wants them to love their neighbour, and that all people are their neighbours. They believe that their love should show in the way they behave, for example by:

- helping people in need

- being friendly to outsiders

- not boasting

- not trying to get their own back on people who hurt them

- being forgiving

- speaking out against things that are wrong and unfair, to try to change things for the better.

They believe that their thoughts, as well as their actions, should be loving and kind.

Some Christians think that the two main things that they should do are help others and tell more people about Jesus and his teachings.

To help them to live as God wishes, Christians pray to God and read and think about the Bible. They believe that Jesus is there to help them as a guide or friend.

Norman is a helper at the Branches Day Centre and Night Shelter for people who are homeless. Local churches set up the centre. They call it 'Branches' because Jesus said: 'I am the vine; you are the branches' (John 15: 5).

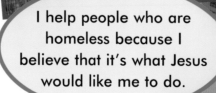

I help people who are homeless because I believe that it's what Jesus would like me to do.

▶ Gillian is an aid worker for the Christian charity Tearfund. She is sent to manage projects in places like Darfur, helping people who have had to flee from conflict. One project is to provide new wells.

My faith makes me believe that everyone should be able to live in freedom and peace, and have access to the food, shelter, healthcare and education that we all need for a happy life. Jesus cared about people's physical needs as well as their spiritual needs, and he asked his followers to do the same.

Difficult questions

What do you think Christians might say about:

- Some new friends have asked me to help them cheat, to make sure we win the prize.

- I'm not speaking to her any more, because she lost the book I lent her.

- I'm worried our street will be spoilt if they build a shelter for the homeless nearby.

- I'm fed up with sorting stuff for recycling. Why should I bother?

▼ What might Christians say about the difficult decisions on page 4? Here is one idea.

I won't buy those trainers. Jesus said not to think so much about clothes and possessions. Also I try to buy fair trade goods, as part of supporting the Make Poverty History campaign.

Beliefs that influence you

Choose one of the situations above. What basic beliefs influence your thoughts about the right thing to do? Write a speech bubble about this to go with a picture of you.

Glossary

archbishop   a very important church leader, in the Roman Catholic, Anglican and Orthodox denominations.

Bible   the holy book of the Christian religion. The first part of it, called the Old Testament, is almost the same as the Jewish Bible.

Bible, Jewish   the scriptures of the Jewish people, made up of three parts. The first part is the Torah, which includes God's laws for his people. The second and third parts consist of books of the Prophets and books of Writings.

campaign   to take part in activities to publicise an issue, with the aim of persuading people to do something about it.

charity   an organisation that works to provide care for people in need. A charity collects money to pay for the care it provides, and to cover its costs, but it does not make profits. 'Charity' also means 'loving care'.

commandment   a religious rule, believed to have been given by God.

conscience   a person's sense of what is right and wrong.

crucifixion   being put to death on a cross, a punishment used in Roman times. Jesus's death is called the Crucifixion.

denomination   a religious group. There are different Christian denominations, such as Roman Catholics, Church of England, Baptists and Methodists.

golden rule   an important idea that guides how to behave. The idea that you should treat others as you like to be treated yourself is known as 'the golden rule'.

gospel   a book in the Bible which tells the life of Jesus. There are four gospels.

honour   to think and feel that someone deserves admiration and therefore to treat them with respect.

hypocrisy   behaving in one way, but thinking, feeling or saying something different or opposite.

inspire   to make someone really want to do something.

Kingdom of God   in Christian belief, where God rules, in people's lives, or in future time.

Levite   an official in the Jewish temple, in the time of Jesus, not as important as a priest.

Lord's prayer   the main Christian prayer, based on what Jesus told his disciples to say when they prayed (Matthew 6: 9-13).

Make Poverty History	a campaign that began in 2005, to persuade governments of richer countries to increase the aid they give to poor countries, to cancel their debts, and to make international trade laws fairer. Find out more from: www.makepovertyhistory.org.	**order**	a religious group whose members live their lives according to a particular set of rules and values.
missionaries	people who are sent to carry out a particular task, often connected with their religion.	**parable**	a short story, or description, designed to show a moral truth.
monastery	a building where a group of monks live and work. (A similar building for a group of nuns is called a convent.) 	**practice**	action. Putting a belief into practice means putting it into action: not just thinking it, but using it in real life.
		Roman Catholic	the Christian denomination that regards the Pope as the head of the Church.
motive	a basic reason, feeling or wish that drives a person to do something or to act in a particular way.	**Samaritan**	a person from Samaria. Today, a Samaritan can also mean a member of the Samaritans, an organisation which took its name from the parable of the good Samaritan. Volunteers for the organisation are always ready to listen on the phone to anyone who needs to talk about their worries.
New Testament	the second part of the Christian Bible, made up of 27 books. The first four are the gospels. They are followed by the book of Acts, which tells how the Christian religion first spread, and then by Letters from early Christian leaders, including Paul.	**sin**	doing wrong or failure to do what is right.
		Ten Commandments	in the Bible (Exodus 20), ten laws given by God to Moses, listing how people should behave to God and to each other.
nun	a woman who devotes herself to her religion, joining a group of nuns, called an 'order'.	**tradition**	a custom that is handed down.
		value	a basic belief about what is important, which influences a person's ideas about right and wrong ways to think and behave.
Old Testament	the first part of the Christian Bible, which is based on the Jewish Bible that Jesus knew. The Old Testament is made up of 39 books.	**vicar**	a priest in charge of a church, in the Church of England.
		volunteer	someone who chooses to do work for no pay, because they want to help.

For teachers and parents

This book has been designed to support and extend the learning objectives of Unit 5D of the QCA Religious Education Scheme of Work and the new QCA Year 6 unit 'How can beliefs and values serve as a guide for moral decision making?'. It moves 'learning about religion' (AT1) from simply knowing about beliefs and practices onto a deeper level of understanding about how such beliefs influence the lives of Christians. It explores the sources of moral guidance, such as the Bible and the teaching and example of Jesus, and the motivation of the love of God which inspires Christians to love their neighbours and their enemies, and to practise forgiveness. It looks at examples of Christian children and adults putting their beliefs and values into practice in real-life situations. This meets the learning objectives 1a, 1b and 1f for Key Stage 2 in the QCA Non-statutory National Framework for RE, as they relate to Christianity, which forms an essential component of every Agreed Syllabus. The book also challenges children to think about difficult decisions in their own experience and to examine their own motivation and value basis for moral choices, so contributing to children's spiritual and moral development and helping to meet the 'learning from religion' (AT2) objectives 2d and 2e for Key Stage 2 in the QCA Non-statutory National Framework for RE. Aspects of this book can contribute to PSHE and citizenship education (2b; 2e; 2h; 4a).

FURTHER INFORMATION AND ACTIVITIES

Pages 4-5 Difficult decisions
Let children imagine a situation where someone has to make a difficult decision and then take turns to 'hot seat' the role, justifying their decision, while others, speaking as 'rules' or 'feelings', etc, try to influence them. Emphasise that there is no simple 'right' answer.

Link to PSHE materials, such as the Tom Snyder CD, *Choices Choices; Taking Responsibility*.

Find out more about the implications of consumer decisions by looking at the websites of companies making the products and emailing firms about their fair trade, environmental or ethical policies. Hold a debate, with groups putting the viewpoint of producer, trader and consumer.

Some good materials are available from OXFAM's 'Cool Planet for Teachers'. See www.oxfam.org.uk/coolplanet.

Pages 6-7 Rules and values
Focus on the class rules and discuss how life might be without any.

Let two groups of children play a new board game, but with only one group having the rules. Then let the groups compare notes.

Ask the children to write a list of the 'unwritten rules' that they and their friends or family usually follow without thinking much about them.

Groups of children can make pictures or collages of a 'behaviour monster' which spoils life for them (for example, the greedy gremlin/anger ogre). Then make 'cages' of rules for the monsters.

RE and ME should not just aim to make children compliant! Discuss various strategies for confronting rules that the children feel are unjust. Investigate examples of wrong rules being challenged by passive resistance, such as Gandhi collecting salt and the story of the dreidel game played at Hanukkah (the game was used to disguise lessons when Jews were forbidden to teach Hebrew to their children).

Pages 8-9 Christian beliefs and values
Compile a fact file of experiences in Jesus's life, using a variety of sources and revising previous learning/general knowledge. Discuss which aspects of his life or teaching Christians today could try to follow.

Be prepared for pupils to bring up controversial Christian beliefs in action, like anti-abortion/homosexuality protests, in discussion of different interpretations of the Bible.

Either invite a Christian to come and explain why Jesus and the Bible are important to them, or investigate this online at REQuest, REJesus and REOnline (>people of faith>email a believer).

Look at pictures of Jesus, as in *Jesus Through Art* by M. Cooling, noticing the emotions in the pictures, and discuss how they help us to get a better idea of what Jesus might have been like. He has been drawn in many different nationalities. Ask the children why.

Examine the Ten Commandments in Exodus 20: 1-17. Which are part of our laws today?

Pages 10-11 What did Jesus say about rules?
In Luke 10: 27, the laws that Jesus quotes are from Deuteronomy 6: 5 and Leviticus 19: 18.

Debate how the seemingly stupid rule of St Augustine, 'Love God and do as you like,' could work in practice.

Jewish rabbis identify 613 mitzvot (commandments) in the Torah (the first five books of the Bible). Attempts at a simple summary, as made by Jesus, were popular. Jesus was a Jew engaged in an 'in-house' debate, so be careful not to stereotype Judaism as legalistic in contrast to Christianity. (For example, Jewish interpretation of 'an eye for an eye' concerns appropriate compensation for loss.)

Ask the children to list ways in which a spiteful person could be unkind to someone, and for each suggestion make a rule forbidding it. Discuss whether this would protect the victim, or whether a change of attitude is needed. How could this come about?

Pages 12-13 Putting beliefs into practice
Let children role-play a range of scenarios where people listen to a speaker talking about moral actions, they all agree and applaud, but some ignore and some act on the ideas.

Jesus's words about a tree and its fruit are in Luke 6: 43-45.

Discuss how far it is true that 'money can't buy happiness'.

Pages 14-15 The parable of the good Samaritan
Read a suitable version of this most well-known Bible story. Be careful that the wording of any retelling does not imply that Jews are the 'baddies', which was not Jesus's point. There is a clear version of the story, with activities, on REQuest (main>bible>goodsam).

Dramatise the story, in a play, a newscast report, or a puppet show. Think about the issues that divide people or make them uncomfortable around each other: religion, politics, homelessness, poverty/wealth, etc. Choose one person to be the injured person, and another to be the good Samaritan. Choose other people to be the ones who ignore the injured person. Reasons for not stopping to help could be: not enough time, not enough money to help, safety worries, might lose their job.

Look at a map showing Jerusalem, Jericho, Judea and Samaria, to see the journey of about 25 kilometres, through rocky desert country.

Show a map of the world, highlighting current disaster areas, headed 'Who is my neighbour?'

Pages 16-17 Why do Christians help the needy?
For an adult-level challenge from the good Samaritan story, see www.op.org/international/english/Documents/masters_order/Radcliffe /samaritan.htm, which shows a Christian applying this story in his life.

Google Mother Teresa and find suitable biographies, pictures and quotation sites to post on an intranet for the children to investigate. Let the class make a display or web page with downloaded pictures, examples and quotations, showing why she did what she did.

Consider whether there are any practical ways in which the class could offer to help people in need. Does the school support a charity or sponsor a child, or is there a current need to which this topic would inspire them to respond?

Pages 18-19 How do Christians help the needy?
Visit a monastery – or ex-monastery! If there is a local one, ask the education officer how children could investigate the ways in which the monastery helped the poor.

Groups of children could investigate and present the stories of great Christian philanthropists. Links to the Victorians can be found from REQuest (main>history). www.barnardos.org.uk explains the basis and values of the charity. www.spartacus.schoolnet.co.uk/REwilberforce gives information about Wilberforce and the abolition of slavery.

Find out what local churches do to help people in need, at home or worldwide. If there is a local charity, ask a representative to come and tell about its work and why they do it.

Pages 20-21 Do to others as you would have them do to you
Give children a card 'coin' which can be tacked either way to the middle of a sheet of paper. On one side of the coin they should draw their own head and write around it, 'How I like to be treated'. On the other side they should write, 'How I should treat others'. Around the coin they can list or draw pictures of behaviour that should apply whichever way the coin is facing. Alternatively, this could be done as a class activity. Challenge 'easy' answers, such as 'being given lots of chocolate', and encourage underlying principles.

If you used the behaviour monsters activity suggested under pages 6-7, extend this to imagine a single 'master key' to lock all the cages and write the Bible verse on a golden key.

Ask the children to write their own name instead of 'love' or 'it' in the verses from 1 Corinthians and use it (privately) as a self-evaluation.

Let the children think about what love means to them and write their own version of 'Love is ...'.

Pages 22-23 Forgiveness
Design a DVD/video box cover for the story of the lost son.

Ask a Christian (for example, musicians or a local church minister) to suggest hymns they like about being forgiven. 'God forgave my sin' or 'I'm forgiven, I'm accepted' show how some Christians may feel. www.hymnal.net has a search facility for hymns and songs.

Pages 24-25 Being forgiving
Get the children to work out 70 x 7. Should we keep a score? Look back to page 21 for a description of the way love treats wrong-doers. Does it mean that people should not be punished for doing wrong?

Refusing to forgive can make people 'hard-hearted'. Does it make them feel better or bitter?

In circle time, discuss the issue of 'getting your own back'.

Pages 26-27 What difference does it make?
List examples of things that people do because of a belief they hold. Encourage the children to relate this to themselves. 'I strongly believe that…., so I do/do not….' (e.g. 'I strongly believe that animals should be respected, so I do not buy products tested on animals.')

USEFUL WEBSITES
QCA: www.qca.org.uk >I am interested in>Subjects>Religious Education>Useful resources
REOnline: www.reonline.org.uk (A 'gateway' RE site with many useful links and a child-friendly junior section.)
REQuest: www.request.org.uk (A wide range of work on Christianity.)
REJesus: www.rejesus.co.uk (An interesting, non-denominational site.)

Index